JOURNAL

Peter Pauper Press, Inc.
White Plains, New York

PETER PAUPER PRESS
Fine Books and Gifts Since 1928

Our Company

In 1928, at the age of twenty-two, Peter Beilenson began printing books on a small press in the basement of his parents' home in Larchmont, New York. Peter—and later, his wife, Edna—sought to create fine books that sold at "prices even a pauper could afford."

Today, still family owned and operated, Peter Pauper Press continues to honor our founders' legacy—and our customers' expectations—of beauty, quality, and value.

Cover image: *Branch of an Almond Tree in Blossom*
Vincent van Gogh, 1890
Van Gogh Museum, Amsterdam, The Netherlands
Art Resource, NY

Peter Pauper Press, Inc.
202 Mamaroneck Avenue
White Plains, NY 10601

ISBN 978-1-4413-0357-8
Printed in China
21